101 Things to Definitely Not Do If You Want to Get a Chick

"Will Forte is a weird dude… It takes courage to be that strange… He is also funny as hell."

—Hollywood legend Jack Black

"In this dating advice book, the first in what he tells me will be a series of 300 advice books that will probably then be made into movies, Will Forte explores romantic relationships with more nuance and tenderness than you would expect if you've ever met him.

"For decades to come, readers will be asking, 'What exactly was wrong with Will Forte?'

"I couldn't love him more if I were paid to.*"

*It's none of your business if I was.

—Tina Fey

"Will Forte has the type of mind that, when studied in a lab, lights up in different colors than a regular person's. In everyday wake mode, he's accessing parts of his brain that are usually only triggered by a lightning strike, an influx of serotonin, or most likely, a salt deficiency. Whatever it is, I hope he keeps thinking outside the outside of the box, because an original like Will needs to be celebrated, protected, pruned, and given ample sunlight and water."

—Paul Rudd

"Will Forte is an American ⸻ those dudes with metal detectors at the beach say that old ⸻ It's all about perspective, really. Also, this book is very silly ⸻

—Andy Samberg

101 THINGS TO DEFINITELY NOT DO IF YOU WANT TO GET A CHICK

WILL FORTE

hachette
BOOKS

NEW YORK   BOSTON

FOREWORD

Hi there! My name is Will Forte and I am the person who drew the dumb little cartoons you're about to look at. For those who DO NOT want to hear the story behind the making of them, turn the page now. For those of you who DO want to hear it, read on!

Okay, before I start, I just want to make sure—do you really want to read this foreword? I'm the one writing it, so I cannot vouch for its quality. I can promise that the grammar will be pretty solid and that everything will be spelled correctley (boom). But the information contained within? Unvouchable. So just take one more moment to think this through—just being a friend here—are you absolutely sure you want to read this foreword?

Take your time. I'll just be sitting here. Tell you what, I'll turn around so you don't feel any pressure.

Just gonna give it ten more seconds...9...8...7...6...5...4...3...2...1...okay, I'm turning back around in 3...2...1...

Oh, hi! You're still here? You want to read the foreword? Great! And, I gotta say, my foreword and I appreciate your support. Okay, let's do this thing!

I (Will Forte) made these cartoons in 1994. At the time, I (Will Forte) was working as an assistant at a music publishing company. My (Will Forte's) job there was—

Okay, I'm gonna stop inserting my name in parentheticals, but for the remainder of this foreword, just assume that every time I say "I" or "me," I'm referring to myself, Will Forte. Okay, back in it—let's do this thing!

So my job at the music publishing company was to make cassette tapes of various songwriters' songs to send out to various big name singers to see if they'd want to record them. In the mid-1990s, the best audio technology at our disposal was a tape-to-tape machine, which meant putting a cassette tape with music in one side, a blank cassette tape in the other side, and then waiting in real time for the songs to record. If I was dubbing one song, I'd be sitting around for about four minutes. If I was dubbing five songs, I'd be waiting around for about twenty minutes. Needless to say, I would get bored pretty quickly and fill the time with various time-wasting techniques. One day, I (Will Forte)...-Oops, sorry, forgot, see previous, sorry again...-I grabbed a napkin and started doodling a picture of a man holding a dead cat as a frowning woman stood across from him. For some reason, I wrote the caption, "Never Kill a Woman's Pets." Suddenly, it struck me that what at first seemed like a stupid little doodle was actually some rock-solid advice. I mean, there are millions of men out there thinking it might be acceptable to kill a woman's pet and then ask her out on a date. But it's not.

And this was a big moment. This was important stuff. I had found my purpose in life. Will Forte, a single, twenty-four-year-old man, who years later would still be single at forty-six, would give men dating advice. I quickly came up with the title *101 Things to Definitely Not Do if You Wanna Get a Chick* and started furiously doodling away. For the next week, cartoons poured out of me. And then the well dried up. But I only had, like, seventy cartoons. And that was a major problem—I mean, the title of this thing was *101 Things to Definitely Not Do if You Want to Get a Chick*. I couldn't change the title. I mean, who changes a title? The only realistic solution was to break my brain coming up with thirty-one more. Sure, the new batch of cartoons might seem too similar to the first batch. Sure, the new batch might be really bad. But there would be 101 of them. And that was important to me. Because who changes a title? Certainly not Will Forte.

Three weeks later, the book was complete. I sent it to a publisher that my father knew. The guy liked the jokes but felt that the drawings were just too crappy to fly. I thought about sending them to another publisher but then pussed out. A few weeks later, I got accepted into The Groundlings Theater and moved on from cartoonistry. That was that, right?

But a funny thing happened as I started working my way through The Groundlings system. The cartoons changed my life.

I sent them to a college buddy of mine (Matt Rice) who had recently become a literary agent. He started sending them around to people. One of these people was a manager (Julie Darmody) who showed them to a producer (Joel Gallen). And the next thing I knew, I had my first professional writing job for the Jenny McCarthy sketch show on MTV. Once that show was over, the cartoons got me my second writing job at *The Late Show with David Letterman*. To this day, one of the most exciting things I've ever heard was that my hero, David Letterman, had seen and liked my dumb little cartoon book. And just like that, I was a working writer and it was all because of the cartoons.

The illustrations might look familiar to some of you. From the KFBR392 notebook in "MacGruber" to my sports ball friends in *The Last Man on Earth*, my drawing style hasn't changed very much. Look, are these things perfect? Absolutely not. Remember, these are basically the first jokes I ever wrote. Just think of them as a snapshot of my brain at the age of twenty-four. If I could go back in time, there are a ton of things I would change. In some of them, I try too hard to be shocking. In some of them, I try too hard to be absurd ("Never Gurd the Blebbner?" WTF?). In some of them, I write past the joke. Some are too offensive. Some too violent. Some just flat out aren't very funny. But some I love with all my heart. I hope you enjoy them. And if you don't, *please* don't tell me—I'm very fragile!

Love,
Will

Do Not Kill Her Pets

Never Reveal Details of Past Relationships

Most women like to believe you've never slapped other women's naked bottoms before.

NEVER TRY TO MILK HER BROTHER

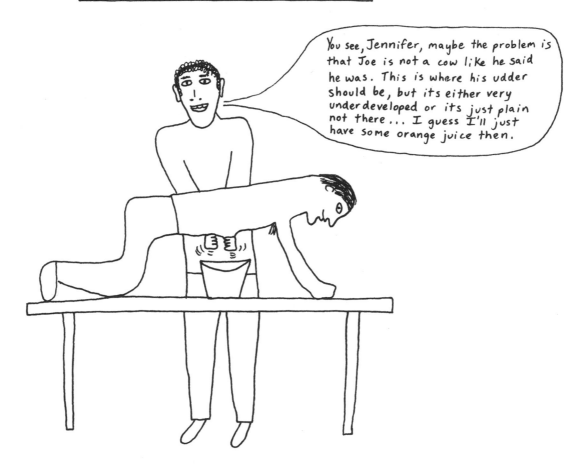

NEVER TATTOO HER FACE ON YOUR FACE

NEVER TRY TO SELL HER FATHER A ROTTEN HAM

NEVER COMPARE HER MOTHER'S BREAST SIZE WITH YOUR MOTHER'S

NEVER STORE YOGURT ON ANY PART OF YOUR BODY FOR NO REASON

Yogurt is a delicious snack enjoyed by many, but, once opened, IT MUST BE REFRIGERATED. Let me reiterate, ONCE OPENED, IT MUST BE REFRIGERATED. A failure to do so would not only highlight a lack of practicality and general health consciousness, but it's just plain dangerous.

NEVER GIVE HER BROTHER A PERM

NEVER INTENTIONALLY DRY HEAVE IN FRONT OF A WOMAN

NEVER MISTAKE HER FOR A HOT DOG

NEVER FORCE HER TO SMELL YOUR FINGER

NEVER MAKE BOOGER ART

NEVER TAKE HER OUT TO DINNER AND ATTEMPT TO PAY WITH A PILE OF FEATHERS

Never Start an Ant Farm on Any Part of Your Body

NEVER CARRY AROUND A WATERMELON FOR A MONTH AND CALL IT DEBBIE

It is normal to want to share all aspects of your life with your special new partner. BUT DON'T PUSH HER TOO QUICKLY. There's plenty of time for her to get to know all of your friends — even Debbie.

NEVER TRY TO TAKE HER TEMPERATURE WITH A CHAIR

NEVER PRETEND YOU'RE A GIANT FORK

NEVER TRY TO GRATE CHEESE WITH HER NOSTRILS

Never Dig for Clams in Her Living Room

Never Take Her to Dinner Dressed as a Figure Skater

NEVER GIVE HER BLOOD FOR CHRISTMAS

NEVER TAKE A GRAVY BATH WITH HER FATHER

NEVER USE HER CREDIT CARD TO BUY 100 POUNDS OF BREAD

NEVER TRY TO SECRETLY MAKE A CEMENT MOLD OF HER FACE

NEVER PRETEND TO BE TRAPPED INSIDE A SPARKLETTS BOTTLE

NEVER LET HER KNOW THAT YOU'VE HAD FOREHEAD IMPLANTS

NEVER HOST AN ALOE VERA CONVENTION AT HER PARENTS HOUSE

NEVER DISGUISE YOURSELF AS A FROZEN TURKEY DINNER

NEVER CONDUCT AN ORCHESTRA ON HER HEAD

NEVER COMPLAIN ABOUT THE BROOMSTICKS
YOU DECIDED TO JAM IN YOUR EYE SOCKETS

NEVER MAKE HER A TOENAIL NECKLACE

NEVER BRAND HER MOTHER

NEVER MAKE FUN OF HEMOPHILIACS IN FRONT OF HER

ON THE FIRST DATE, NEVER SHOW HER YOUR BED AND EXCLAIM,

"THIS IS WHERE I WILL FATHER OUR CHILDREN!"

NEVER TURN YOURSELF INTO A BUSH

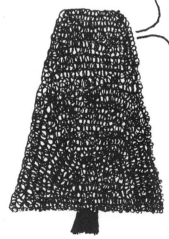

.... my arms, branches to hold you ... my eyes, two green leaves ... impossibly green, but not the green of envy ... the green of growth and fertility ... Yes, Jennifer, now I'm a bush and there's nothing I can do to change that .... but I still feel the emotions of a man ... I'm a bush that laughs, a bush that cries .... a bush that loves.

Never Scold Her Kitchen Utensils

NEVER EXPOSE OLD GRUDGES

NEVER USE ONLY PRONOUNS WHEN TRYING TO HOLD A CONVERSATION WITH HER

NEVER PLAY THE AIR PIANO

Never Argue with Her Mirrors

NEVER SECRETLY JAM A "PARK YOUR CAR HERE FREE" SIGN IN THE BACK OF HER FATHER'S NECK

NEVER HITCHHIKE FROM HER LIVING ROOM TO HER KITCHEN

NEVER REVEAL YOUR NAME WHEN CRANK CALLING HER PARENTS

NEVER HIRE A SKYWRITER TO CONVEY YOUR FEELINGS

NEVER TAKE BOARD GAMES TOO SERIOUSLY

NEVER BUILD A MASHED POTATO CASTLE ON HER CAR

NEVER TALK CLEAN TO HER OVER THE PHONE

NEVER MAKE HER A PAIR OF LEOTARDS OUT OF YOUR OWN SKIN

NEVER CLAIM TO HAVE THE POWERS OF THE SUN

NEVER INTRODUCE HER AS YOUR WIFE ON YOUR FIRST DATE

NEVER TREAT HER FATHER LIKE A SUPER MODEL

Okay, now give me the pouty look like you're saying, "Ooooooooo, I'm gonna get whatever I want" .... Now turn it into a smile ... gently ... Oh that's hot .... now throw your hips out and your hands up in the air like you don't have a care in the world ... Oh Mr. Carter ... sell it .... sell it .... Oh that's hot, sir.

NEVER BRAG ABOUT GOING TO HIGH SCHOOL WITH HARRISON FORD

NEVER GURD THE BLEBBNER

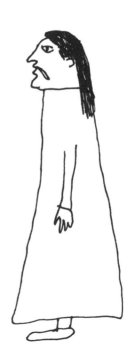

NEVER SCALP YOURSELF AND GIVE IT TO HER LIKE A BOUQUET

Special Witch Doctor Section

Never Pour the "Juice of the Hells" on Her Father's Head

NEVER SECRETLY GET HER NAME CHANGED

Other Possible Names:

Vargelm Torg Carter
Igorm Wendy Carter
Jelatin Christina Carter
Turtle Loaf Carter
Gentle Benna Carter
Bo and Luke Duke Carter
Bulb Tennis Carter
Ruby Corn Carter
Jerdren Phleb Carter
Piñata Tina Carter
Plate of Lasagna Carter
OR JUST
Gurg

NEVER CHALLENGE HER BROTHER TO A STITCHERY DUEL

NEVER TAPE HER MOTHER GOING TO THE BATHROOM

NEVER NAME YOUR BOAT AFTER HER MOTHER

NEVER BUY A WOMAN A HERMAPHRODITIC RHINOCEROUS

NEVER CLAIM TO HAVE COLLABORATED WITH A FAMOUS POET

Never Ice Her Father's Nipples

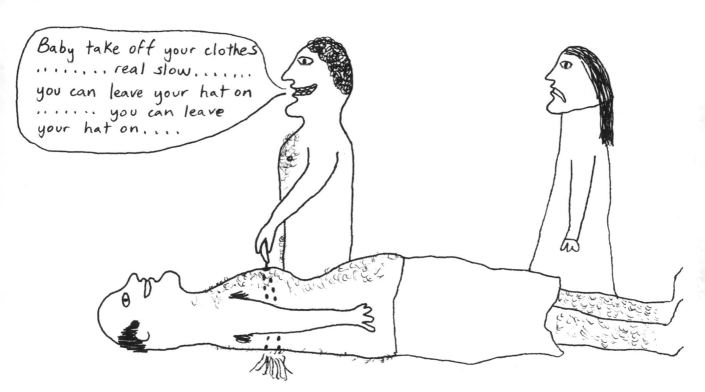

NEVER EXPLAIN YOUR NICKNAME TO HER PARENTS

NEVER TRY TO SELL HER PROPHYLACTICS FROM THE BACK OF A VAN

Hachette Books
Hachette Book Group
1290 Avenue of the Americas
New York, NY 10104
hachettebookgroup.com
twitter.com/hachettebooks

First Edition: October 2016

Hachette Books is a division of Hachette Book Group, Inc.
The Hachette Books name and logo are trademarks of Hachette Book Group, Inc.

The publisher is not responsible for websites (or their content) that are not owned by the publisher.

The Hachette Speakers Bureau provides a wide range of authors for speaking events. To find out more, go to www.hachettespeakersbureau.com or call (866) 376-6591.

Library of Congress Control Number: 2016946597 ISBNs: 978-0-316-46419-2 (trade paperback), 978-0-316-46420-8 (ebook)

Printed in the United States of America

10 9 8 7 6 5 4 3 2 1

33614057770017